COUNT ON

1

Grow vocabulary by:

- **Looking** at pictures and words
- **Talking** about what you see
- **Touching** and naming objects
- **Using** questions to extend learning...
  Ask questions that invite children
  to share information.
  Begin your questions with words like...
  who, what, when, where and how.

2

3

These books support a series of educational games by Learning Props.
Learning Props, L.L.C., P.O. Box 774, Racine, WI 53401-0774
1-877-776-7750 www.learningprops.com

Created by: Bev Schumacher, Learning Props, L.L.C.
Graphic Design: Bev Kirk
Images: Hemera Technologies Inc., Bev Kirk, Matthew 25 Ministries

Library of Congress Control Number 2004092048   ISBN 978-0-9741549-6-1

LEARNING PROPS

1

one

finger

baby

bear

2

two

fingers

shoes

apples

3 three

ice cream cones

peppers

4 four

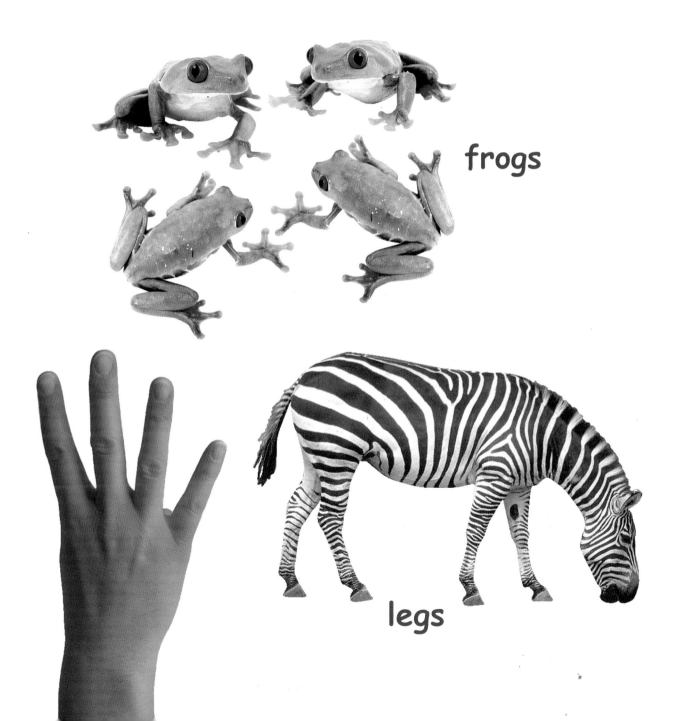

frogs

legs

5 five

children

glasses

six

6

scissors

kittens

7 seven

birthday gifts

balls

8

eight

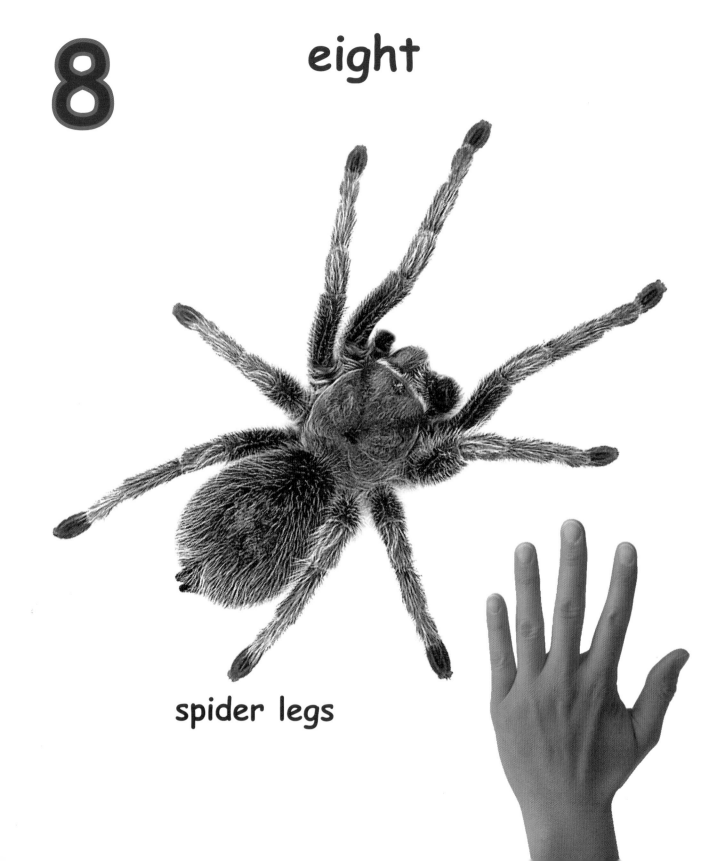

spider legs

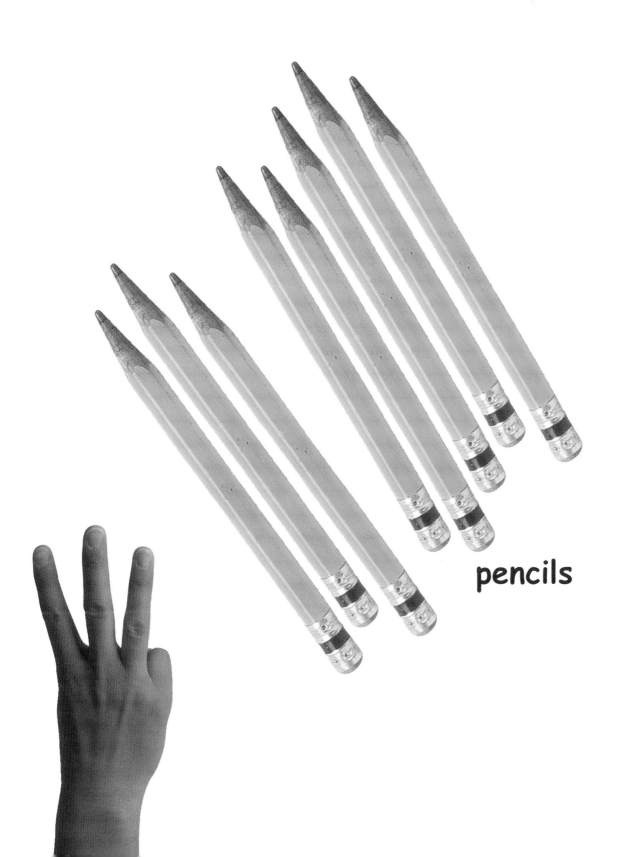

pencils

9

nine

bunnies

fish

10 ten

dinosaurs

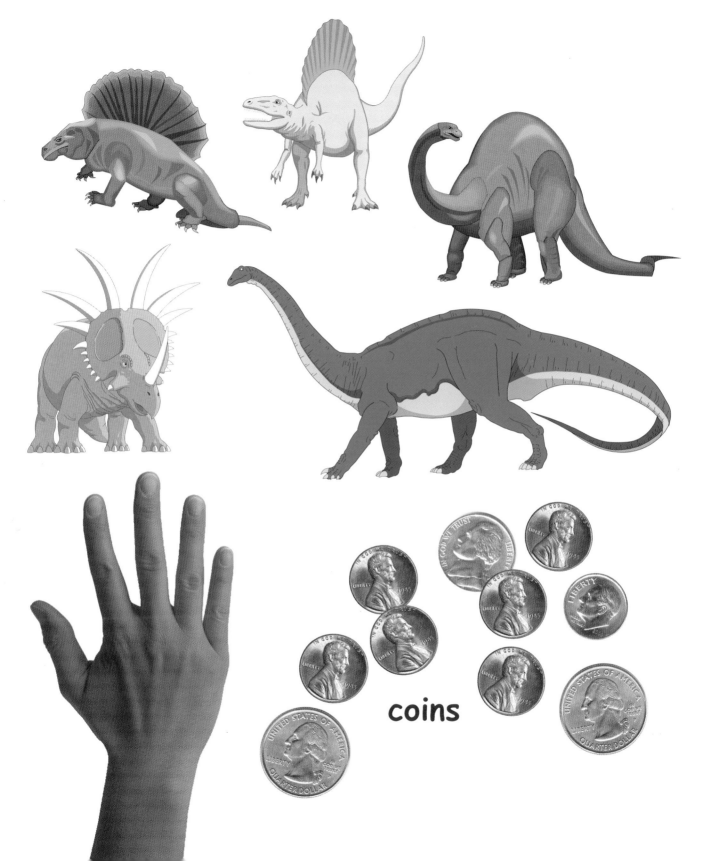

coins

eleven **11**

twelve **12**

thirteen **13**

fourteen **14**

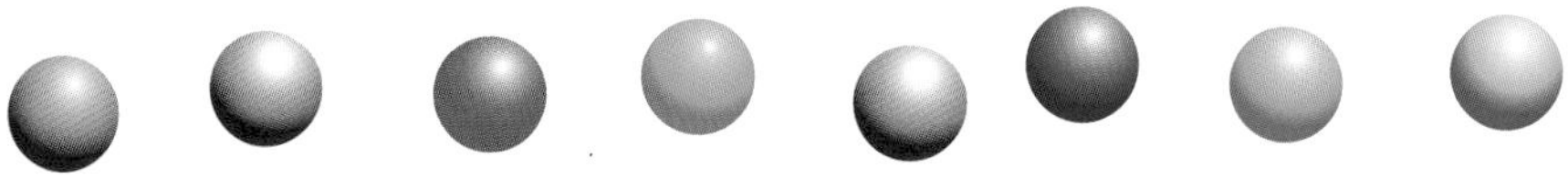

fifteen **15**

sixteen **16**

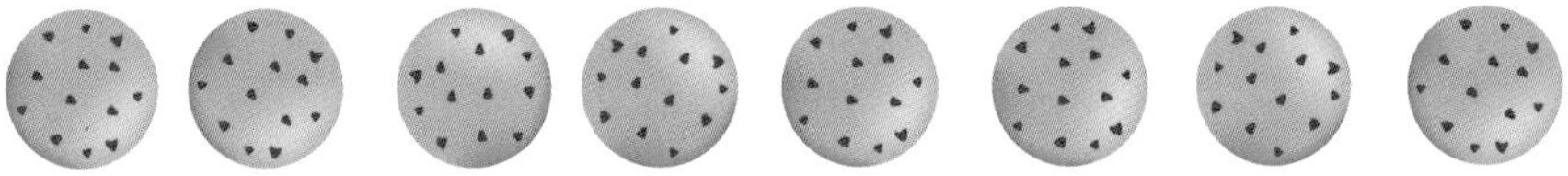

seventeen **17**

eighteen **18**

nineteen **19**

twenty **20**

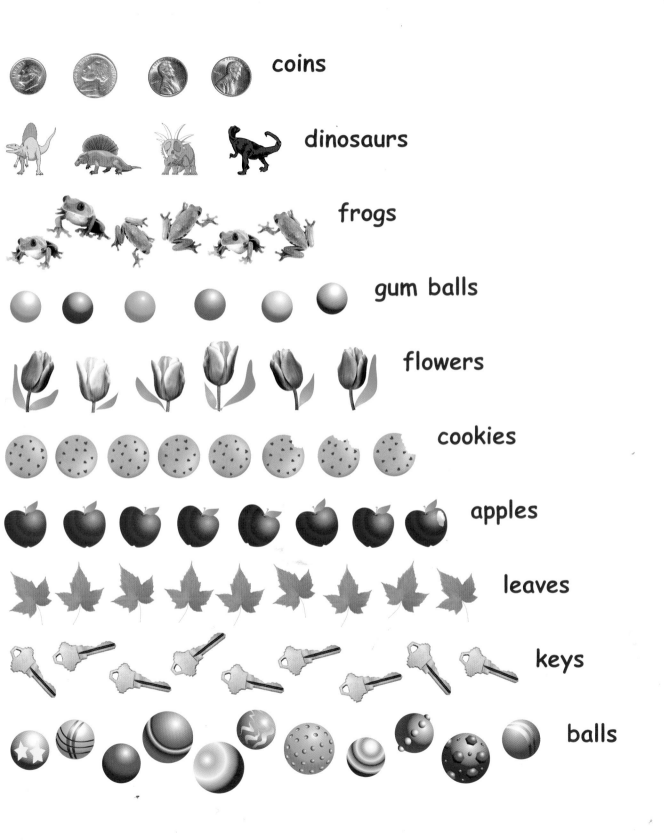

coins

dinosaurs

frogs

gum balls

flowers

cookies

apples

leaves

keys

balls

find the numbers

1
2
3
4
5
6
7
8
9
10

pronunciation

Count On Me! / **Kount On Mee!**

find the numbers / **finde** THuh **nuhm**-burs

1 one / **wuhn**
2 two / **too**
3 three / **three**
4 four / **for**
5 five / **five**
6 six / **siks**
7 seven / **sev**-uhn
8 eight / **ate**
9 nine / **nine**
10 ten / **ten**
11 eleven / ee-**lev**-uhn
12 twelve / **twelv**
13 thirteen / **thur-teen**
14 fourteen / **for-teen**
15 fifteen / **fif-teen**
16 sixteen / **siks-teen**
17 seventeen / **sev**-uhn-**teen**
18 eighteen / **ate-teen**
19 nineteen / **nine-teen**
20 twenty / **twen**-tee

apples / **ap**-uhls
baby / **bay**-bee
balls / **bawls**
bear / **bair**
birthday gifts / **burth**-day **gifts**
bunnies / **buhn**-ees
children / **chil**-drin
coins / **koins**
cookies / **kuk**-ees
dinosaurs / **dye**-nuh-sors
finger / **fing**-gur
fingers / **fing**-gurs
fish / **fish**
flowers / **flou**-urs
frogs / **frogs** *or* **frawgs**
glasses / **glass**-iz
gum balls / **guhm bawls**
ice cream cones / **eyess kreem kohns**
keys / **kees**
kittens / **kit**-uhns
leaves / **leevs**
legs / **legs**
pencils / **pen**-suhls
peppers / **pep**-urs
scissors / **siz**-urz
shoes / **shooz**
spider legs / **spye**-dur **legs**